Saints
CHRONICLES
Collection 4

SOPHIA INSTITUTE PRESS
Manchester, NH

SOPHIA
INSTITUTE PRESS

Text and Images Copyright © 2018 Sophia Institute

Printed in the United States of America.

Sophia Institute Press®
Box 5284, Manchester, NH 03108
1-800-888-9344
www.SophiaInstitute.com
Sophia Institute Press® is a registered trademark of Sophia Institute.

Names, persons, places, and incidents featured in this publication are based on historical fact but have been subject to author and artist discretion for dramatic purposes. All text, except when specifically cited, has been written by the author, not to be mistaken for actual historical documentation.

The Saints Chronicles Collection 1, ISBN: 9781622826742
The Saints Chronicles Collection 2, ISBN: 9781622826766
The Saints Chronicles Collection 3, ISBN: 9781622826797
The Saints Chronicles Collection 4, ISBN: 9781622826803

Library of Congress Cataloging-in-Publication Data

Title: The saints chronicles. Collection 1. Saint Patrick, Saint Jerome Emiliani, Saint Elizabeth Ann Seton, Saint Henry Morse, Saint Joan of Arc.
Description: Manchester, NH : Sophia Institute Press, [2018]
Identifiers: LCCN 2018038952 | ISBN 9781622826742 (pbk. : alk. paper)
Subjects: LCSH: Christian saints–Biography–Comic books, strips, etc. |
   Christian martyrs–Biography–Comic books, strips, etc. |
   Catholics–Biography–Comic books, strips, etc. | Patrick, Saint, 373?-463?
   –Comic books, strips, etc. | Jerome Emiliani, Saint, 1486-1537
   –Comic books, strips, etc. | Seton, Elizabeth Ann, Saint, 1774-1821 .
   –Comic books, strips, etc. | Morse, Henry, Saint, 1595-1645
   –Comic books, strips, etc. | Joan, of Arc, Saint, 1412-1431
   –Comic books, strips, etc. | Graphic novels.
Classification: LCC BX4655.3 .S255 2018 | DDC 282.092/2 [B] –dc23
LC record available at https://lccn.loc.gov/2018038952

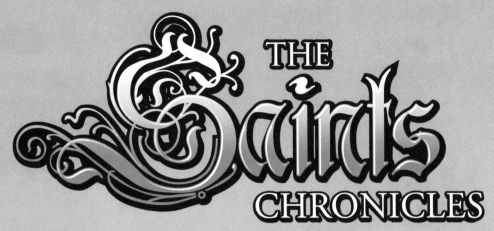

THE Saints CHRONICLES

Collection 4

Which friends are you willing to work with side by side in sharing Christ with others?

SAINT WILLIBRORD

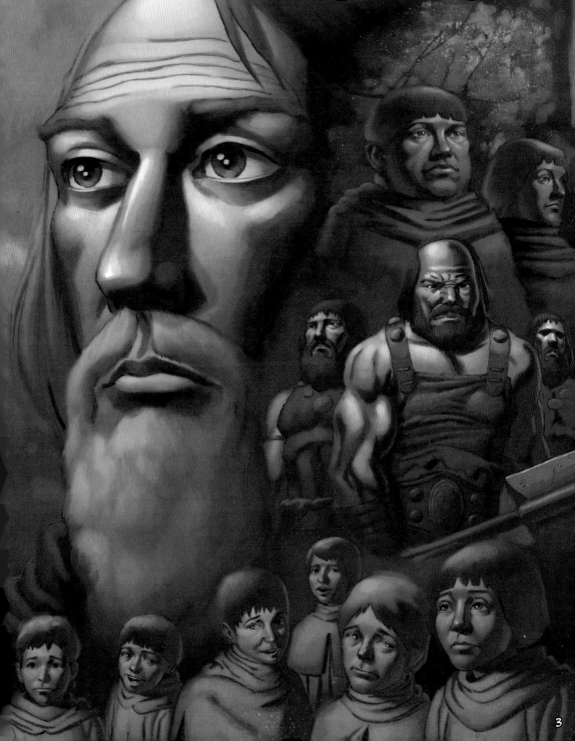

SAINT WILLIBRORD

The Prayer of St. Willibrord:

O Lord our God, who call whom you will and send them where you choose: We thank you for sending your servant Willibrord to be an apostle to the Low Countries, to turn them from the worship of idols to serve you, the living God; and we entreat you to preserve us from the temptation to exchange the perfect freedom of your service for servitude to false gods and to idols of our own devising; through Jesus Christ our Lord, who lives and reigns with you and the Holy Spirit, one God, for ever and ever. "

ST. WILLIBRORD WAS ONE OF THE FIRST ENGLISH MISSIONARIES TO SPREAD THE GOSPEL. AT THE AGE OF SEVEN, HIS FATHER SENT HIM TO A MONASTERY FOR STUDY AND ENLIGHTENMENT. A MERE EIGHT YEARS AFTERWARD, THE TEENAGE WILLIBRORD WAS A SCHOLAR AND BENEDICTINE MONK.

BY HIS TWENTIETH YEAR, HE BEGAN TO TRAVEL, GOING FIRST TO IRELAND FOR ADDITIONAL STUDIES. ORDAINED AS A PRIEST A DECADE LATER, WILLIBRORD ACCEPTED THE HOLY CALLING TO WORK AMONG THE GERMANIC PAGANS OF THE PROVINCE OF FRIESLAND IN THE NETHERLANDS.

POPES BLESSED HIM. WORLD LEADERS SOUGHT HIS ADVICE. HEATHEN KINGS FEARED THE TRUTH OF JESUS CHRIST AND THE LIGHT OF THE LORD THAT WILLIBRORD BROUGHT INTO THEIR MIDST.

IN ST. WILLIBRORD'S WAKE WERE CHURCHES, MONASTERIES, AND THOUSANDS UPON THOUSANDS OF SAVED SOULS. HIS WAS A LIFE WELL LIVED AND WELL SERVED. HE DIED PEACEFULLY AT THE AGE OF EIGHTY-ONE WITH THE TITLE "APOSTLE OF THE FRISIANS."

Producer	Editorial	Story	Art	Letters	Design
Daniel Burton	Kimberly Black	Terry Collins	Jason Millet	Keith Bahrenburg	Brad Jones

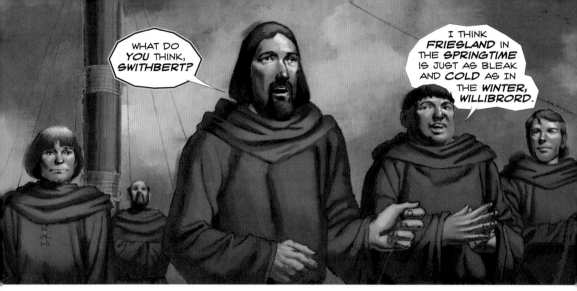

WE MIGHT JUST *GET OUT* OF THE NETHERLANDS IN *ONE PIECE* AFTER ALL!

SO, YOU'VE MADE IT TO THE *CASTLE OF UTRECHT*.

WHAT IS IT THAT *BRINGS* YOU TO THE COURT OF THE *CAROLINGIAN EMPIRE?*

WE ARE *HUMBLE MISSIONARIES*, GOOD KING, WHO WISH TO SPREAD *THE GOSPEL* OF THE PRINCE OF *PEACE* TO YOUR FAIR LANDS.

PEACE IS A *PRECIOUS COMMODITY*, FATHER WILLIBRORD.

STILL, IF PEACE IS WHAT YOU ARE *SELLING*, THEN BY ALL MEANS *BRING YOUR WARES* TO THE PEOPLE.

I *ENCOURAGE* YOU TO TRAVEL LOWER FRIESLAND. YOU HAVE *MY PERMISSION* TO PREACH BETWEEN THE *MEUSE** AND *THE SEA*.

BUT, *BE WARNED*. MANY ARE STILL *LOYAL* TO *RADBOD* AND WANT TO SEE HIM RECLAIM *THESE TERRITORIES* AS HIS OWN.

* THE MEUSE: A RIVER IN WESTERN EUROPE THAT FLOWS FROM FRANCE THROUGH BELGIUM AND THE NETHERLANDS TO THE NORTH SEA.

RISE, MY SON.

YOUR **HOLINESS**, I HAVE MET WITH KING PEPIN OF **HERSTAL** AND HAVE RECEIVED HIS PERMISSION TO BRING **THE GOSPEL** TO THE PEOPLE OF **LOWER FRIESLAND**.

I HAVE COME TO **ROME** TO BEG YOUR BLESSING IN **THIS ENDEAVOR**.

NOW -- WHAT BRINGS **YOU** FROM **THE NETHERLANDS** TO ROME **THIS DAY**?

WILLIBRORD, YOU **NEED NOT** BEG. ALL YOU HAVE TO DO IS **ASK**, AND YOUR REQUEST **SHALL** BE GRANTED.

I GIVE YOU **AMPLE** JURISDICTION TO SPREAD **THE WORD**, AND YOU SHALL BE **GRANTED RELICS** FOR THE CONSECRATION OF **CHURCHES**.

YOUR **MISSIONARIES** GO WITH MY **FULL BACKING** AND AUTHORITY.

8

FINALLY! WERE YOU GRANTED AN AUDIENCE WITH POPE SERGIUS?

YES. YES INDEED.

YOU ARE TRULY BLESSED, FATHER WILLIBRORD! WHAT DID HIS HOLINESS SAY?

HE SUPPORTS US FULLY AND AGREES THAT GOD IS WITH US IN OUR TASK, HOBBERT.

SO FROM IRELAND TO THE NETHERLANDS TO ROME. WHERE'S OUR NEXT STOP?

NO MORE DETOURS, MY FRIENDS! WE CAN FOCUS ON THE TASK AT HAND AT LAST!

MUCH TIME HAS BEEN LOST ALREADY IN TRAVELING, SWITHBERT. ONCE WE ARRIVE ON THE SHORES OF LOWER FRIESLAND, WE MUST MAKE HASTE.

EVEN WITH **KING PEPIN'S DECREE** TO TRAVEL FREELY, WE MUST BE BOLD AND MAKE OUR **PRESENCE KNOWN.**

ONCE THE PEOPLE **SEE THE LIGHT** OF THE LORD, THEY WILL JOIN US IN OUR **MISSION.**

BE ASSURED, SWITHBERT. WE BRING THEM TRUTH AND **GUIDANCE.**

FOR THEM TO **ACCEPT** US IN THEIR **MIDST,** THE PEOPLE **MUST KNOW** OUR INTENT IS PURE.

WE SHALL ESTABLISH OUR **FIRST CHURCH** WITHOUT DELAY.

ONCE WE HAVE **A BASE,** WE CAN **DIVIDE OURSELVES** AND MOVE DEEPER INTO THE HOMES AND **THE HEARTS** OF THE **GOOD PEOPLE** OF FRIESLAND.

WHEN *I* GAVE YOU LEAVE TO TRAVEL THE LANDS OF *LOWER FRIESLAND* YEARS AGO,

NEVER DID I EXPECT YOU TO MAKE *SO MUCH* PROGRESS -- AND *SO QUICKLY!*

I *DID NOT* DO IT ALONE, KING PEPIN. WITHOUT ALL OF *THE MISSIONARIES* WHO --

YES, YES, I KNOW. BUT *AN ARMY*, EVEN ONE AS SMALL AS YOURS, MUST HAVE *EFFECTIVE GUIDANCE.*

YOU *GOVERN WELL*, WILLIBRORD. THE SKILL OF *LEADERSHIP* IS A GREAT GIFT.

I *UNDERSTAND* YOUR FRIEND HAS GONE *ELSEWHERE?*

YES, AFTER BEING CONSECRATED AS BISHOP BY *WILFRID OF YORK*, SWITHBERT TRAVELED UP THE RHINE TO *PREACH* TO THE BORUCTVARI.

SPEAKING OF TRAVEL -- I NEED YOU TO MAKE *A JOURNEY* ON *MY* BEHALF.

ME? BUT I HAVE *SO MUCH* TO DO *HERE!*

EVEN SO, *WILLIBRORD*, YOU MUST GATHER YOUR *BELONGINGS* AND PREPARE TO *RETURN TO ROME.*

I FELT I WAS **NOT WORTHY** OF SUCH A **GREAT HONOR.**

BUT **RATHER** THAN BE STUBBORN, I **ACCEPTED** THE RESPONSIBILITY.

YOU, STUBBORN? **NEVER!**

YOU **ONLY STAYED** IN ROME FOR **FOURTEEN DAYS,** FATHER -- ER, I MEAN, **BISHOP** WILLIBRORD.

I WAS **ANXIOUS** TO RETURN, HOBBERT.

CHRISTIANITY IS SECURE WITHIN THE BOUNDARIES OF ROME, WHILE MUCH WORK **STILL REMAINS** INCOMPLETE HERE IN FRIESLAND.

I **BELIEVED** OUR WORK TO BE **FINISHED** WITH THE FRANKS.

IN THE **LOWER HALF** WE HAVE MADE **GREAT STRIDES.** WE MUST NOW PUSH FORWARD, INTO **UPPER FRIESLAND.**

THAT LAND IS **STILL** UNDER THE RULE OF **RADBOD,** UNLESS YOU HAVE **HEARD** OTHERWISE.

NO, BUT **I** GROW **WEARY** OF FEARING A MAN I HAVE **NEVER EVEN MET.**

SO **WHAT** ARE YOU GOING TO **DO?**

TAKE A -- **DIRECT** APPROACH.

13

I WILL ADDRESS **KING RADBOD** MYSELF AND MAKE MY CASE TO OFFER **GOD'S SALVATION** TO HIS **PEOPLE**.

YOU ARE **WILLIBRORD?**

YES, AND THANK YOU FOR **SEEING** ME, KING RADBOD.

I AM **MANY THINGS** BUT NEVER AN **UNGRACIOUS** HOST.

WHAT DO **YOU** WANT FROM A SO-CALLED "**HEATHEN**" RULER, HOLY MAN?

I WANT TO OFFER YOU THE **WORD OF LIFE.**

ONCE I HAVE **RECAPTURED** THAT WHICH IS **RIGHTFULLY** MINE, YOUR GOD WILL BE **BANISHED** FROM MY KINGDOM!

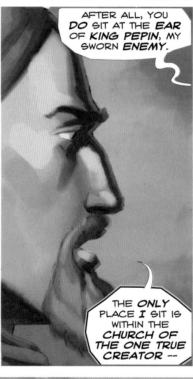

AFTER ALL, YOU **DO** SIT AT THE **EAR** OF **KING PEPIN,** MY SWORN **ENEMY.**

THE **ONLY** PLACE **I** SIT IS WITHIN THE **CHURCH OF THE ONE TRUE CREATOR** --

PRIEST, **YOUR GOD** IS NOT **MY GOD.** I WISH YOU NO ILL WILL, BUT **KEEP YOUR DISTANCE** WITH YOUR TEACHINGS.

IF **YOUR GOD** IS INDEED THE **ONE TRUE CREATOR,** WE SHALL SEE WHO IS SAVED AND **WHO FALLS.**

YES, KING RADBOD -- **WE SHALL.**

MY GUARDS WILL SEE YOU BACK **ACROSS** THE BORDER.

DO NOT COME HERE AGAIN.

14

My dear Swithbert, I hope this letter finds you in good health and spirits.

I fear my attempt to reach out to the king of Upper Friesland bore no fruit. To trespass on Radbod's lands would be a death sentence.

Undeterred, we moved forward to the Land of the Danes and met with their ruler, a man known as Ongendus: a man with a heart of stone.

His people were steeped in evil practices, abandoned to idolatry, and indifferent to any hope of a better life … but in their children I saw hope and brought those willing back with me to the land of the Franks.

On our long ocean voyage, I instructed the youths in the faith --

In case they were to perish from the long sea voyage or through the ambushes of the savage dwellers of these parts.

I will write again when I have more news to share.
Your loyal friend in Christ,
Willibrord

GOD WAS WITH US. THE DAMAGE ISN'T *BAD*, SO WE CAN MAKE REPAIRS AND CONTINUE ON *OUR WAY* IN A FEW DAYS.

THAT IS *GOOD NEWS*, BUT I FEAR YOU ARE NOT TELLING ME THE *ENTIRE STORY*, HOBBERT. WHAT IS *WRONG*?

I HAVE *HEARD* OF THIS ISLAND, AND ITS *PURPOSES*. THIS SO-CALLED PLACE OF WORSHIP IS A *DEVOTION* TO A PAGAN GOD KNOWN AS *FOSITE*.

THE *RULER* ON THIS ISLE MUST *BE CLOSE*. I HAVE HEARD HE DOES *NOT GO FAR* FROM THE TEMPLE, SO HE CAN SEEK *DAILY GUIDANCE*.

WHAT DO YOU *WANT TO DO*, BISHOP WILLIBRORD?

WE MUST **TAKE CAUTION,** BISHOP WILLIBRORD. THIS PLACE, THIS **ISLAND** -- IT IS A LAND REVERED **AS HOLY** BY BOTH THE DANES AND THE FRISIANS.

YOU MEAN WE'VE **RUN AGROUND** IN HELIGOLAND? **HOW** DO YOU **KNOW?**

WHEN I WENT TO **HIGHER GROUND** TO GET OUR BEARINGS, I DISCOVERED **A TEMPLE.**

WORDS **FAIL ME.** YOU MUST SEE IT WITH YOUR **OWN EYES.**

BRING THE **OTHERS** FROM THE SHIP TO ME. **BRING THEM ALL.**

AS PROMISED, THE PAGAN KING INDEED CHOSE A MEMBER OF MY PARTY -- AND WITHOUT HESITATION, TOOK HIM FROM US.

I PROTESTED BUT WAS MOCKED IN REPLY.

I POINTED OUT THAT I WAS THE ONE WHO HAD USED THE FOUNTAIN, BUT I WAS TOLD TO WATCH AND SEE WHAT SWIFT JUSTICE THEIR AWFUL, STONE GOD DEMANDED.

POOR, GOOD, BRAVE HOBBERT. NOT ONCE DID HE BEG FOR MERCY.

HE SAVED HIS WORDS FOR GOD AND GOD ALONE.

WHAT SAY YOU NOW OF YOUR GOD, HOLY MAN?

I URGE YOU, GOOD KING -- LET ME BAPTIZE YOU SO THAT ALL YOUR SINS MIGHT BE WASHED AWAY, THAT YOU COULD ENJOY EVERLASTING GLORY WITH GOD.

IT IS CLEAR TO ME THAT MY THREATS LEAVE YOU UNMOVED.

THEN, HE TURNED AND WALKED AWAY.

SO THE KING LET YOU RETURN TO THE CHURCH OF THE SAVIOR HERE IN UTRECHT?

I HAVE TO BELIEVE MY FAITH, AS WELL AS HOBBERT'S, DID NOT GO UNNOTICED AND THAT THE SEED OF FAITH WAS PLANTED DESPITE THE KING'S REACTION.

HOBBERT WORE THE MARTYR'S CROWN WITH GRACE, BISHOP WILLIBRORD.

COME, YOU SHOULD REST AFTER SUCH A TRYING VOYAGE.

SOON, MY FRIEND. SOON ENOUGH.

LORD, I HAVE NEVER WAVERED IN MY DEVOTION, BUT THE PAGAN KING SUCCEEDED IN MAKING ME ASK THE QUESTION --

WAS IT MY PRIDE THAT CAUSED HOBBERT TO DIE ON THE ALTAR OF A FALSE GOD?

SOMEDAY, WHEN MY WORK IS TRULY FINISHED, I HOPE AND PRAY I WILL FIND AN ANSWER.

ON *THIS* DAY, MY MIND RETURNS BACK TO *MY YOUTH*. MY FATHER, AS A *DEVOUT* YOUNG MAN, MARRIED MY MOTHER *EARLY* IN HIS LIFE.

THEY *WANTED* A SON. *THE LORD* HEARD THEIR PRAYERS, AND *I* WAS *HIS* REPLY.

AS SOON AS I WAS *OLD ENOUGH*, MY FATHER PRESENTED ME TO THE *MONASTERY OF RIPON* WHERE I STUDIED AT THE FEET OF *WILFRID*.

THUS *BEGAN* MY JOURNEY ON *THE PATH* TO ENLIGHTENMENT.

I AM *READY* TO JOIN GOD IN THE *PLACE* HE HAS PREPARED FOR ME -- FOR *ALL OF US*.

I NEVER *TRULY KNEW* MY FATHER, BUT I *LOOK FORWARD* TO JOINING HIM AND *MY MOTHER* -- AND HOBBERT, AND ALL THE SOULS THAT HAVE BEEN *TOUCHED*.

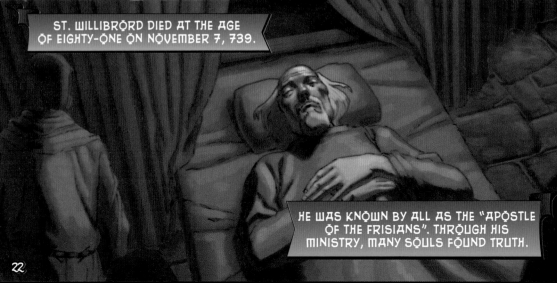

ST. WILLIBRORD DIED AT THE AGE OF EIGHTY-ONE ON NOVEMBER 7, 739.

HE WAS KNOWN BY ALL AS THE "APOSTLE OF THE FRISIANS". THROUGH HIS MINISTRY, MANY SOULS FOUND TRUTH.

SETTING SAIL

c.658 WILLIBRORD IS BORN IN NORTHUMBERLAND (NORTHEASTERN ENGLAND). HIS BIRTH IS A BLESSING TO BOTH HIS PARENTS.

665 HIS FATHER TURNS OVER HIS SON AT THE AGE OF SEVEN TO SERVE THE MONASTERY OF RIPON, WHERE THE BOY'S STUDIES ARE CLOSELY WATCHED AND ENCOURAGED BY ST. WILFRID.

678 A TRUE ADVENTURER, RELENTLESSLY DRIVEN TO SPREAD THE WORD OF GOD, WILLIBRORD TRAVELS TO IRELAND FOR FURTHER STUDY.

689 WILLIBRORD IS ORDAINED A PRIEST.

690 WITH HIS FRIEND SWITHBERT AND TEN OTHER MISSIONARIES, WILLIBRORD TRAVELS INTO FRIESLAND, A PROVINCE OF THE LOW COUNTRIES THAT SURROUNDS THE MOUTH OF THE RHINE RIVER. SOME WARRIORS OF THE LAND WELCOME THE TRAVELERS, WHILE OTHERS REJECT THE TEACHINGS OF THE MONKS AND THE TRUE GOD THEY REPRESENT.

695 POPE SERGIUS I ORDAINS WILLIBRORD BISHOP OF THE FRISIANS.

695-705 WILLIBRORD CONTINUES HIS MISSIONARY WORK IN NORTHERN FRIESLAND AND THE SURROUNDING AREAS. WHILE AT UTRECHT, WILLIBRORD ESTABLISHES MANY SCHOOLS AND CHURCHES. HE ADVISES ROYALTY AND THE COMMONERS ALIKE.

716 RADBOD, THE RULER OF SOUTHERN FRIESLAND, RECLAIMS PARTS OF HIS LANDS TO THE NORTH, UNDOING MOST OF WILLIBRORD'S WORK.

719 RADBOD DIES, AND WILLIBRORD RETURNS TO PREACH THROUGHOUT FRIESLAND. HE IS COMMONLY PROCLAIMED TO BE THE "APOSTLE OF THE FRISIANS."

739 HE LABORS UNCEASINGLY AS BISHOP FOR MORE THAN FIFTY YEARS, BELOVED BY BOTH GOD AND MAN, AND DIES NOVEMBER 7TH AT THE AGE OF EIGHTY-ONE. WILLIBRORD IS BURIED IN THE MONASTERY OF ECHTERNACH IN LUXEMBOURG.

Will you lead your family and those around you in doing God's work?

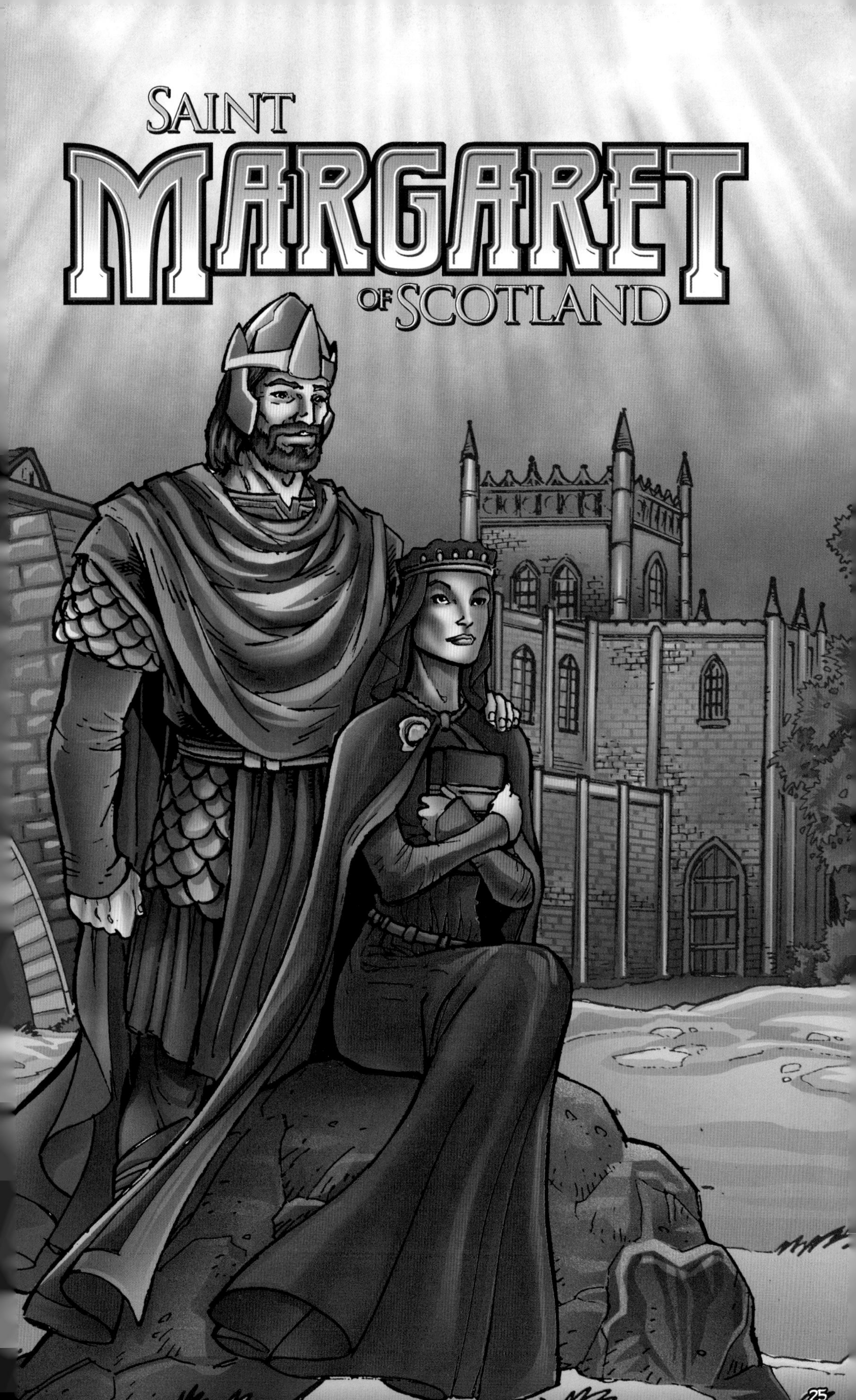

SAINT
MARGARET
OF SCOTLAND

SAINT MARGARET OF SCOTLAND

Every day each one of us is presented with choices. These can be as easy as choosing what color shirt to wear or as hard as telling on a friend for doing something wrong at school.

A deeper decision might offer this choice: Do I strive to do the right thing or turn a blind eye to a person in need?

The harder path is to assist our fellow man, but it is also a path that leads to a richer reward.

St. Margaret grew up within the arms of royalty, but as a child she was devoted to God.

As she matured into adulthood, she believed her path would lead her to becoming a nun.

But God had other plans for Margaret, and presented her with a choice of either following her desire to join a convent ... or allowing herself to love a king in a foreign land, to do the Lord's work with her husband's blessing and backing.

God always presents us with choices.

This is the story of how Margaret made hers.

PRODUCER:
DANIEL BURTON

EDITORIAL:
KIMBERLY BLACK

STORY: TERRY COLLINS

PENCILS: RON LIM

COLORS:
DANIEL BURTON

LETTERS:
KEITH BAHRENBURG

DESIGNS:
KEITH BAHRENBURG
& AARON COOK

On the run and *exiled* without a country to *call* home.

First *Hungary*, then England ... and now we are adrift a *third time*, seeking shelter once more.

Cursed be the name of *William the Conqueror!*

Will his *lust* for power *ever* be *filled?*

Christina, it does little good to curse *any man, no matter* his deeds.

Perhaps William will someday *return* our homelands to us.

In *any event*, he will be *held accountable* for his *actions.*

SLAM!

There's *no fleeing* this storm -- we're *off course* and coming up on *rocky terrain!*

Land, you say? Where *are* we, Edgar?

The *captain* says it looks like we're approaching *Scotland*, Mother. And more quickly than *anyone* would like.

Scotland? Do you expect us to **consort** with those unruly savages, Edgar?

Do you **really**?

I **don't** think we **have much** in the way of **choice**.

OOF!

I **don't** want to go to **Scotland!** I want to go back -- AIEEEEE!

Ooohhh ...

Shhh ... it will be **all right,** sister!

Water ... so cold....

Take my **hand!** Hold tight.

Christina? **Are you awake?**

Don't be scared, sister. **I'm** right by **your** side. I **won't** leave you.

We **must** have **faith.**

Wake up, Christina ...

You've *been sleeping* for nearly *two days*, child.

You are *well*, sister. As always, *the Lord* provides.

Where *are* we?

The Royal Burgh of Dunfermline, about three miles from the *Bay of Forth*.

As I asked *before*, 'Where are we?'

We're in *Scotland*, of course. Not far from *the coast*. After the *ship* hit the *rocks*, we made our way *inland*.

The *good people* of this land saw our *dress*, and believed us to be of the *Scottish Royal Court*.

You've awakened within the *castle* walls of *King Malcolm the Third*.

Edgar is meeting with him *now* to discuss our *fates*.

I *share* your family's *pain* of being *exiled*, Prince Edgar.

I, *too*, lost my home when *my father* was murdered by *Foul Macbeth*.

The *throne* was seized when I was *a child*. I was swept away, to wait my *chance to return*.

When I was *of age*, I *killed* the *false usurper* of the crown and took my *rightful* place *as king*.

These are *dangerous* times, and allies are *to be treasured*. I have *not* forgotten the kindnesses I received within the *Saxon court of Edward the Confessor*.

I propose *an alliance* against William the Conqueror and will grant you *safe haven* in this time of need.

You are *most generous*, kind King.

Are **we** the **only** ones dining **this** evening?

Yes. I wanted to speak with you **privately.**

King Malcolm, while I **appreciate** your generosity, I must question **your** motives.

Why have I been **singled** out from **the rest** of my family? Is my brother playing **match-maker** behind my back **again?**

You have **nothing** to fear, **Fair Margaret.** However, if it is a chaperone you wish, I can summon **your mother**, the good Lady Agatha, and --

No, no -- it **isn't** that.

What is it then?

Frankly, I'm not sure what you're **trying to do** here. I'm hardly impressed by **wasteful habits.**

Wasteful? **Nonsense!** This table is set in **your** honor.

Then you **need** to **rethink** how you **honor a woman.** Good night, **sire.**

I *didn't* mean to *upset you.*

I'm hardly *upset.* *Annoyed* is more like it. How *many* people in the town below are going *hungry* tonight?

You *dare suggest* I keep my subjects *hungry?*

What I *suggest* is *thinking* before taking such *foolish actions* as preparing a royal banquet for *only two people.*

Heh. You say *what you think,* don't you?

Speaking the *truth* is always *best,* wouldn't you *agree?*

I could *use* such *honesty* in my *court.* Perhaps your *temporary* stay could become *more permanent.*

Well, I suppose there is *much good* I could do with the *powers of a monarch* at my back.

As a *queen,* you could accomplish even *more.*

Aye, if I *loved* a king.

Perhaps in time *you* will.

April, 1070. Easter Sunday.

Four years later.

I can't *believe* this day is *finally* here!

Oh *Lord*, what *joy* you have given me in King Malcolm. Though this is *not the life* I planned, Lord, you had *better* in mind.

You know I had *every* intention of leaving the *world of royalty* far behind *after* fleeing *England*.

And now, I live in a Scottish *castle* and have fallen *in love* with a *king*.

Sister, everyone is *gathered* and waiting. *Are you ready?*

I am, sister -- I am.

My *wedding day!* Such a *far cry* from my earlier *plans* of becoming *a nun!*

Today I live my life as a *queen* instead of within *the walls* of a *convent.* Such a *different path* You have *given* me to follow.

Margaret? *You're* up early -- I could have *slept all day* after the wedding reception *last night.*

I *never* sleep more than *a few hours.*

My mind is *always thinking,* you see ... and I have much to *accomplish* during my first week *as queen.*

Thank You, God, for *showing* me there are *different ways* to offer *service* in Thy name.

Thank You for *the gift* of such a *good* and *loving husband* as Malcolm.

You should allow yourself *to rest*. Even God Himself wants *His* children to *sleep*.

And *I* shall, but *not* just yet.

Then *I* will rise and *stay up* with you.

Together, we can accomplish *twice as much*.

Summer, 1070.

Another book, my lady?

Scripture, Malcolm.

Ah, **yes**. Part of your **daily meditations**.

Margaret, I have **never** known another to **adore books** as **much** as you.

Books hold **great truths**, husband. I do wish **you would** take the time to **read**.

Anything that **you** hold so precious **is worthy** of the attentions of **a king**.

I **kiss** this book in honor of your **grace** and **wisdom**, Margaret.

And before you now, I **confess** ... I do **not** know **how** to read.

Then **I** will **teach you**.

Winter, 1070.

Sire, it is with a *heavy heart* I must tell you that your *new bride* is *not* to be trusted.

In *fact*, she is consorting with *enemies from England.*

WHAT?! Is this some sort of *dark jest?* My wife's heritage is *known by all.*

Her *family* was driven from English shores by the *same accursed Norman* that wars with us *now!*

King Malcolm, I *do not* make these accusations *lightly.*

Often in *your absence*, the queen creeps out of the castle, *alone* and unescorted.

Passersby have *seen her* enter *the cave* at the edge of the woods and *heard her talking* to another within.

Enough.

I will *not* believe such claims without seeing with my *own* eyes!

I will *announce* a royal hunt tomorrow, but *stay behind* at the castle *in secret*.

When Margaret *leaves*, I will *follow* her into this "*cave of betrayal*."

And if what these *evil tongues* say is true, then my wife *will not* live to betray Scotland *another day*.

Lord of all ... I *pray to you*.

Teach my dear husband, *king* of these lands, to *serve* Thee truly.

August, 1075.

Five years later.

Sire, *before* we arrive at the construction site, I *must* talk with you about *the queen.*

The *treasury* is constantly being *emptied* by *her projects.* You must *put a stop* to --

If *you* have a problem with what *she is spending,* take the matter up with *the queen herself.*

I will hear *no more* talk of withholding money from the *good* and *charitable* work Margaret does in the name of *our Creator.*

Her *word* is *law* in all *domestic affairs.*

The builders are *on schedule,* I see.

Yes, but since I see *Donald* at your side, I wonder if I'll have *enough money* to pay them for their *labors.*

Er, *no*, my Queen ... there are *ample funds* to complete the building of this *grand abbey.*

Ample?

Yes! Lots! *Plenty!*

How go the talks *with England?*

England is as *stubborn* as ever, *but so are we.* This truce is temporary *at best.*

Donald was wondering if you had another *charity* in need of *support.*

Yes! As always, the royal treasury is at *your disposal.*

Well ... since we are *blessed* with *healthy children* of our own, my thoughts turn to the *orphans* of Scotland.

I believe it is *our Christian duty* to offer *assistance.*

Each morning, I wish to have *nine orphan babes* brought to my rooms.

I will **serve** them **personally**, and **bless** them.

And **monthly**, we shall open the **doors** of the castle to **hundreds** of the downtrodden and serve them with **food** and **fellowship**.

By such **actions**, we demonstrate the power of **God's love**.

I shall **begin** preparations **immediately**, my Queen.

See that **you** do ....

Thank **you**, good Donald.

Margaret, you have made me the **happiest man** in all of Scotland. You have **softened** my temper, **polished my manners** ... presented me with **a son**.

I **thank God** for you **every day**.

And I **thank God** for bringing you into **my life**, Malcolm.

I never knew I was **missing** a piece of myself until I **found** you.

HEAVEN-SENT

Circa 1045 Margaret is born. She is raised in Hungary, where she learns to read the scriptures in Latin. Born a royal, she is trained in French customs and matters.

1050-1060
Margaret spends most of her youth in the court of her great-uncle, the English king Edward the Confessor.

1066 Due to war and strife, Margaret and her family flee England for the safer lands of Hungary. On the way, a storm causes their ship to land in Scotland instead, where they are welcomed as friends by Malcolm III.

1070
King Malcolm and Margaret are married.

1070-1080 Scotland undergoes a religious and cultural renaissance via the influence of Queen Margaret.

Nov. 12, 1093
Malcolm is slain in battle along with Edward, his son and heir.

Nov. 16, 1093 Already ailing, a devastated Margaret dies a mere four days after learning of the death of her child and her beloved husband.

1250
Margaret is canonized by Pope Innocent IV.

1673
Margaret is declared Patroness of Scotland.

1693
Pope Innocent XII declares November 16, the anniversary of her death, to be Margaret's feast day.

How prepared are you to show courage in the face of great evil?

Saint Stanislaus

INTRODUCTION

Born at **Szczepanow**, Poland on July 26, 1030, St. Stanislaus was raised to be devoted to **God**. For years his parents had **tried** to have a baby **without** success. They **considered** his birth a **gift from heaven** and knew he was destined for **great things**.

As an **adult**, his preaching brought about a **spiritual revival** among his congregation, and people from **all walks** of life sought out **his** advice. Being a man **generous** to the poor and successful in bringing about **religious reforms**, St. Stanislaus was consecrated as a bishop in 1072.

Each one of **us** is **challenged daily** to stand up for what we believe. Nearly a thousand years ago, St. Stanislaus **took a stand** and **ultimately** paid the price with his own life for defying the orders of a **king**. You might ask, "**Why did he make this sacrifice?**" The answer is because it was the right thing to do. His belief in **God** is what gave him the strength to face the **challenges** brought before him.

Today, St. Stanislaus is recognized in **Poland** as a **martyr**, dying for speaking out against the evils of the **cruel King Boleslaus**.

This is his story.

PRODUCER:
DANIEL BURTON

EDITORIAL:
KIMBERLY BLACK

STORY:
TERRY COLLINS

PENCILS:
KEVIN WEST

INKS:
DAN DAVIS

COLORS:
JAMES BROWN

LETTERS & DESIGNS:
KEITH BAHRENBURG

They will **return!** The **King** will not be **far** from **his** royal **guard!**

I **know** ...

Then you must leave, **Bishop Stanislaus**. There's a wagon waiting nearby with **fresh horses** and --

And **where** would you have me **go?** My place is **here**, my **son**.

Serving the Lord is my **privilege** and **duty**, as it has **always** been since the day of my **birth**.

My parents discovered their **wealth** was of **no use** when trying to have a child. So they **prayed** for a **baby** ... and, after many years, their faith **was rewarded** with the **gift** of a **son**.

My parents considered **my birth** to be a **miracle**. As such, I was encouraged in **every way** to be **faithful** to the **Lord**.

As I grew into **adulthood**, I **knew** I wanted to **serve God** as well as the men and women in **His** care.

I was **educated** in the city of **Gnesen**, where I studied the **ancient texts** and words of our **faith**.

Lampert Zula, then the bishop of **Kracow**, ordained **me** as a priest. And so it was then that I intended to spend **my years** in **service** to Christ and His **Church**.

Understand, **control** is important to men such as **Boleslaus**. The desire to dominate **fuels** their lives ...

as well as their **desires**.

Who is that **beautiful** woman?

I believe she is **Basha**, King **Boleslaus**, wife to the nobleman **Jarek**. They were wed **last fall**.

Jarek, you say?

An OUTRAGE!

Driver, **STOP** the carriage.

My **liege**, I really don't **think** --

Then we are in **agreement**. I **don't** want you to **think!**

What is **wrong?** I have done nothing.

Oh, I **disagree**, my dear. You **have caught** my attention, and **my heart**.

The King **KNOWS** of the **scandal** his conduct has **caused**.

He **KNOWS**, but does he **REALIZE** the **impact** it is having on his **people?**

Of course he does, but you see? **He doesn't care.**

His **cruelty** and desires are established. Are you **prepared** to fully withstand his **rage?**

I **SEE** ... that is what I **thought**. However, **do not** fear. I will **again** approach the **king** as **your emissary**.

Bishop Stanislaus, I will **stand with you**. I am begging for your **help**.

He took **Basha**, my wife, from me, Bishop. **My wife!** **How** can that be **just?**

No, Jarek, the king's actions are **not just**. There **is** a final way I **can** rebuke him -- I can bring about the **full reproach** of the Church.

Horses approach! The soldiers are back. *This time*, they've brought the *king* himself!

Then *open* the doors and bid him *welcome*.

How *DARE* you launch a formal sentence of *excommunication* against me, Bishop!

I am here to seek *an apology* for such insult.

You were *warned*, King Boleslaus. Your sins have *brought* about these events and --

Speak not to me of sins, you *pathetic* **WRETCH!**

This morning I was late to Mass. I **knew** I had **missed** the public prayer of the Church, the **entrance procession**, the veneration of the altar --

but I **still** came.

Word had **reached** me of your **plans** to keep me **out** of the **cathedral**, Stanislaus.

Thanks to **you**, my presence was now required at **Mass** to show my subjects **I** would **not** be **censured**.

But **then** I entered the **Cathedral of Kracow** this morning to find what? **WHAT?**

Maybe **The Liturgy of the Word?** Or a washing of hands?

No. What I found was a cathedral **filled** with **people**, yet all was **still**.

It was **almost** as if they were ...

waiting for me to **appear**.

King Boleslaus, by order of the **Holy Bishop of Kracow**, these services are suspended upon your having been **excommunicated!**

My **liege**, you are no longer **welcome** within the walls of **this**, or **any**, church!

I **could not** believe what I was **hearing**. I was no longer **welcome?**

Surely, there **must** be some mistake ... **some error** in judgment.

So **here** I am, **Bishop** Stanislaus, waiting to hear what **you** have to say before I **pass judgment** on **you**.

When I **returned from war** in triumph, **beloved** by all ... celebrated by **not just** a city, but by an **entire country** ...

I was a **hero**, respected in word and **renowned in deed.**

I was **not surprised** when I was named **King of Poland.** No one objected; the **masses** were happy.

But since the **first** day of my leadership, **you** have **opposed** me.

No king, you forget. I was **also there** when you were crowned, and **I approved.**

Then why have you **forsaken** me?

It is **not I,** but **you** who have forsaken the **Church,** a good Christian life, **and yourself.**

BAH! You **don't** understand the pressures of leadership -- **you never did.**

Pope Alexander *himself* even had to *insist you accept* the post as *Bishop of Kracow* after the *death of Lampert Zula.*

Titles are *meaningless* to the *Lord.* Did my work with the poor *vary?* *No*, it did not.

Did *my efforts* for the diocese *alter? No*, they did *not.*

Leadership *does not* give you the right to *use your station* as *an excuse* for bad behavior.

Excuses? I make neither *excuses* nor apologies for *my actions!*

But *even* in those times, *you came* and *prayed with me!*

How *often* did *I* approach you with warnings that *you* had *gone too far* -- had pushed the people past what *they* could *withstand?*

LEGEND HAS IT THAT THE PEOPLE ROSE UP AGAINST THE MURDEROUS KING AND DROVE HIM FROM THE BORDERS OF POLAND BUT THAT IS NOT TRUE.

HOWEVER, THERE IS NO DOUBT THAT THE KING'S ACTIONS HASTENED HIS FALL FROM POWER. FLEEING POLAND, BOLESLAUS WAS LATER TO SERVE PENANCE WITHIN THE WALLS OF A HUNGARIAN MONASTERY.

THREE DAYS AFTER HIS DEATH, BISHOP STANISLAUS WAS BURIED AT THE DOOR OF THE CHAPEL IN WHICH HE WAS SLAIN.

THE BISHOP'S EXAMPLE AND BRAVERY SHOW US ALL THAT WE MUST STAND UP BOLDLY AGAINST EVIL, DESPITE THE CONSEQUENCES ...

NO MATTER THE ODDS ...

NO MATTER THE PRICE.

ST. STANISLAUS WAS THE CHAMPION OF THE LIBERTY OF THE CHURCH AND THE DIGNITY OF MAN. HE DEFENDED THE RICH AND THE POOR, NO MATTER THEIR STATION OR BACKGROUND. HE IS THE PATRON SAINT OF POLAND.

A BRIGHT LIGHT

Born at Szczepanow, Poland on July 26, 1030

St. Stanislaus studies in Paris

St. Stanislaus is ordained a priest by the bishop of Kracow, Lampert Zula.

St. Stanislaus is consecrated as a bishop in 1072 by Pope Alexander II.

St. Stanislaus excommunicates King Boleslaus.

St. Stanislaus dies at the hand of Boleslaus on April 11, 1079

In 1253, Pope Innocent IV canonizes St. Stanislaus as the first Pole ever to be Canonized.

How has God's plan for you been different from your parent's plan for you?

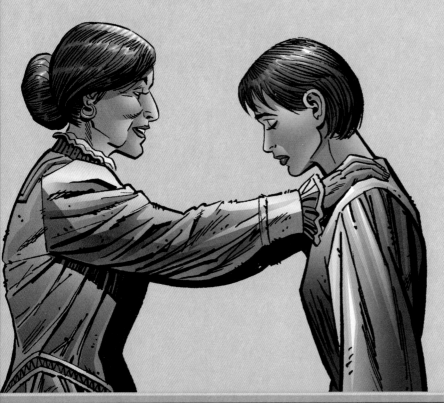

SAINT
ROSE OF LIMA

69

PRODUCER
Daniel Burton
EDITORIAL **Kimberly Black**
STORY **Roger Brown**
PENCILS
Tod Smith INKS
Al Milgrom
COLORS
Mark McNabb
LETTERS & DESIGN
Jeff Dawidowski

Young Isabel had most everything society admires today: beauty, grace, admiration, attention. In today's culture, we exalt material wealth and selfish ambition; and for Isabel, a life of physical indulgence was not only possible, but probable.

But though young "Rose," as she came to be known, possessed these worldly assets, she was never seduced by them. Instead, Rose bravely stood against the materialistic, choosing in its place a life of spirituality, suffering, and sacrifice. St. Rose of Lima denied worldly goods for holiness, relinquishing the body she had never been comfortable with at the young age of thirty-one. Because of this, she is honored for her great piety and faith.

So which life would you have chosen?

Follow the remarkable tale of St. Rose of Lima, and see just how this small girl who became a devout woman transformed a family, a town, a country, and a faith.

SON, STAY WITH THE HORSE -- I MUST GO TO YOUR *MOTHER!*

OLIVIA!

LORD, PLEASE PROTECT MY WIFE ...

IS SHE -- ARE THEY --

HUSH, NOW, FOR ALL IS WELL.

SAY HELLO TO YOUR BABY DAUGHTER.

MY DAUGHTER ...

AND *OLIVIA,* HOW IS SHE?

YOUR WIFE IS FINE, BUT SHE NEEDS TO REST.

THE DELIVERY WAS A *SUCCESS,* BUT YOUR DAUGHTER WAS BORN *EARLY.* HER HEALTH MAY BE IN *JEOPARDY ... THIS* YOU MUST KNOW.

LORD, YOU HAVE BLESSED US WITH A MOST *BEAUTIFUL* CHILD.

YOUR *BODY* MAY BE WEAK, LITTLE ONE, BUT I *PRAY* THAT YOUR WILL TO LIVE BE STRONG.

Her father's wish for young Isabel was granted and, miraculously, she survived. As the years passed, she grew in both body and spirit and soon found her beauty renowned across the land.

Praised by friends and strangers, pious Isabel was embarrassed by such attentions; why couldn't the rest of the world see what she saw -- the beauty the Lord had put in every soul?

WHAT A *LOVELY* CHILD.

SHE HAS TO BE THE MOST *BEAUTIFUL* CHILD IN ALL OF *LIMA!*

WHY, SHE'S AS *BEAUTIFUL* AS A *ROSE!*

But the people had spoken, and in Isabel's Confirmation ceremony of 1597, she was renamed "Rose" in honor of her great delicacy and beauty.

ROSE, DARLING --

THANK YOU, LORD, FOR THE BLESSINGS YOU HAVE GIVEN *ME* AND *MY FAMILY*. BRING THEM PEACE.

BLESS ME AND KEEP ME. I AM ALWAYS YOURS. YOU HAVE MY HEART AND SOUL *FOREVER*. AMEN.

But Rose's beauty was nothing compared to her devotion to the Lord. Even at the tender age of five, her parents could not help but notice that Rose's heart had but one love: God.

73

One morning, while attending Mass, Rose sought out her priest to ask him a most important question.

GOOD MORNING, ROSE. YOU ARE LOOKING *BEAUTIFUL*, AS ALWAYS.

THANK YOU, AND GOOD MORNING TO YOU, MS. ANITA.

SURELY THE PRIEST WILL BE ABLE TO HELP ME.

FATHER?

YES, MY CHILD.

I LONG TO GIVE MY *LIFE* IN SERVICE TO THE *LORD*, BUT I AM WORRIED ABOUT MY APPEARANCE.

DO YOU THINK THE LORD WORRIES AS WELL? WOULD MY BEAUTY GET IN THE WAY OF SERVING HIM?

GOD BELIEVES THAT *ALL* OF HIS CHILDREN ARE *BEAUTIFUL*, ROSE. HE HAS CREATED *YOU*, AND HIS CREATION IS *NOTHING* TO BE ASHAMED OF!

THANK YOU, FATHER -- YOU HAVE BEEN MOST *HELPFUL!*

After returning home, Rose knew she had one last thing to do to ensure people would take her devotion to the Lord seriously ...

SNIP! SNIP!

75

One day, many years later, while Rose was in town with her father, she was yet again inspired into action.

FATHER, THESE PEOPLE *SHOULDN'T* HAVE TO LIVE THIS WAY ...

I *AGREE*. IT SADDENS ME TO SEE PEOPLE SUFFER.

I HAVE *HIRED* AS MANY OF THEM AS POSSIBLE TO WORK THE MINES, BUT THERE ARE STILL THOSE IN *NEED*.

GOD, YOU HAVE *BLESSED* US IN SO MANY WAYS. PLEASE SHOW ME WHAT ELSE I CAN DO TO *HELP* THOSE LESS FORTUNATE ...

AND HELP ME TO EXTEND THAT SAME *LOVE* AND *COMPASSION* TO OTHERS ... AT ALL TIMES.

HERE, LET ME *HELP* YOU WITH THAT!

BLESS THESE *CHILDREN*; SHOW THEM YOUR UNENDING *LOVE* AND *COMPASSION*.

MAY GOD *BLESS* YOU, CHILD, FOR HELPING AN OLD WOMAN.

I HAVE BEEN WALKING WITH THE LORD FOR MANY YEARS NOW, AND ALL I *WISH* IS TO DO HIS BIDDING.

LIMA IS INDEED BLESSED TO HAVE YOU AMONG US, DEAR.

I AM AFRAID IT IS TIME TO *RETURN* HOME, ROSE. I KNOW YOU WOULD RATHER *STAY*.

YES, FATHER, I WOULD. BUT I FEEL IN MY HEART MY WORK IS NOT YET DONE IN THIS PLACE.

BEAUTIFUL, ISN'T IT? YOUR *GRANDMOTHER* GAVE THAT TO ME AS A WEDDING GIFT *YEARS* AGO.

SPEAKING OF ...

ROSE, I THINK IT IS TIME WE TALKED ABOUT YOU CONSIDERING A *HUSBAND*.

YOU *MUST* DESIRE A HOME, A FAMILY OF YOUR *OWN*. YOU ARE WELL KNOWN, AND AS SUCH, YOU WOULD HAVE *YOUR* CHOICE.

BUT MOTHER, I CAN'T *MARRY!*

I AM *ALREADY* MARRIED TO MY FAITH.

I KNOW HOW *DEVOTED* YOU ARE TO GOD, AND *NOTHING* COULD MAKE ME HAPPIER. BUT IT WOULD PLEASE US *GREATLY* IF YOU WOULD *TRY* TO DO THIS.

I DESIRE *ONLY* YOUR *HAPPINESS* ... MY FAMILY HAS BROUGHT ME MUCH *JOY*, AND I WISH THAT FOR *YOU* AS WELL.

I UNDERSTAND, MOTHER, YOUR WISHES FOR MY LIFE. I WILL TRY -- BUT PLEASE KNOW I CANNOT PROMISE YOU THE RESULT YOU SEEK.

True to her mother's word, a suitor arrived the next day.

I WANT TO **THANK YOU**, SIR, FOR ALLOWING ME TO SEE YOUR DAUGHTER. I HAVE ALWAYS **ADMIRED** HER BEAUTY AND GRACE.

YES, ... YES, SHE IS A **VERY** SPECIAL CHILD. COME INSIDE; HER **MOTHER** WILL LET HER KNOW YOU ARE HERE.

ROSE, YOU LOOK **BEAUTIFUL!**

REMEMBER, MOTHER, I SAID I WOULD **MEET** THIS MAN. NOTHING **MORE,** NOTHING **LESS.**

WELL, LET'S JUST SEE WHAT **HAPPENS.** I'LL GO DOWNSTAIRS AND TELL HIM YOU'RE COMING.

WHO KNOWS? HE MAY SURPRISE YOU.

HMMM ... PEPPERS.

THE **PERFECT** TOUCH!

PLEASED TO **MEET** YOU!

ROSE!

IT IS MY ... UH ... PLEASURE ... I ...

PLEASE, SIR -- *WAIT!*

PLEASE FORGIVE ME FOR WHAT'S HAPPENED, BUT I ONLY WANT TO SERVE THE *LORD.*

I HAVE DECIDED TO JOIN A *CONVENT!*

THAT IS OUT OF THE *QUESTION!* CAN'T YOU FIND A WAY TO SERVE THE LORD AND *STILL* BE NEAR US?

PLEASE, ROSE, *PRAY* ON IT TONIGHT, AND LET US DISCUSS IT *LATER.*

Rose prayed into the morning, asking the Lord for an answer.

And indeed she received it.

OF COURSE! WE WOULD *LOVE* YOU TO BECOME A MEMBER OF THE THIRD ORDER OF *ST. DOMINIC.*

WONDERFUL!

BROTHER, DO YOU SEE THAT VACANT PORTION OF OUR FATHER'S LAND?

I WISH TO BUILD A *SMALL SHELTER* UPON IT TO USE IN MY *SERVICE* TO THE PEOPLE OF LIMA. CAN YOU *HELP* ME?

I WOULD BE *PROUD* TO HELP YOU, LITTLE SISTER. IT WON'T TAKE LONG AT *ALL!*

THIS WILL ALLOW ME TO SERVE THE PEOPLE OF *LIMA* AS I HAVE *DREAMED* WHILE BEING CLOSE TO HOME.

THANK YOU, MOTHER. I WILL SERVE THE LORD AND THE PEOPLE OF LIMA *FAITHFULLY.*

And so Rose's family helped make the small house that would serve as her place of prayer and healing for the people of Lima. She was right; she started serving the townspeople in no time at all.

She even walked the streets of her beloved city, praying for those who had wandered far from the Lord. But her peaceful days of prayer were soon to be interrupted ...

THE TOWN IS UNDER *ATTACK!* DUTCH PIRATES HAVE COME ASHORE! WE MUST LEAVE **QUICKLY!**

PIRATES? HURRY, CHILD, **SHOW ME!**

IT IS TRUE -- THEY HAVE ARRIVED! I MUST DO SOMETHING ... BUT WHAT? LORD -- GIVE ME GUIDANCE!

CRASH

Br-DOOM

After that day, Rose became an advocate for the people of Lima. Not only did she help to save her town from pirates but also from a kingdom oceans away which threatened to compromise their very livelihoods.

AS I HAVE **PLEADED** WITH THIS COURT **MANY** TIMES, IT IS AGAINST **ALL** THAT IS **MORAL** THAT THESE PEOPLE WORK THEMSELVES TO **DEATH** SO THE PURSES OF **SPAIN** CAN BE FILLED WITH **GOLD.**

ALL I ASK IS THAT A **PORTION** OF THEIR **HARD** WORK BE GIVEN **BACK** TO THEM SO THAT THEY CAN LIVE A **DECENT** LIFE!

IS IT NOT IN **GOD'S** WORD THAT WE SHOULD TREAT **OTHERS** AS WE WOULD BE TREATED?

I DO NOT THINK THE **ROYALS** OF SPAIN WOULD WANT TO BE DEALT WITH IN THIS **MANNER** -- SO WHY WOULD WE ALLOW THEM TO DEAL WITH OTHERS THIS WAY?

For the rest of her life, Rose fought for reform for the people of Lima, and they loved her for it.

But soon Rose became gravely ill.

People from all over the town of Lima took turns caring for her ...

... just as she had taken care of them.

And then, at the tender age of thirty-one, Rose went on to be with the Lord she loved so much.

Though Rose lived a short time on this earth, her deeds and love for the Lord live on today. Her body rested in a Dominican convent until it was later moved to a special chapel in the church of San Domingo, where it rests to this day.

the Life of Rose

1586 Rose is born and christened "Isabel" in Lima, the capital of Peru, to parents Caspar de Flores and Maria del Olivia.

St. Toribo, Archbishop of Lima, confirms the name "Rose" to the small girl, and she is forever known as such.

Rose admires St. Catherine of Siena and begins to disfigure her physical beauty, going so far as to rub her hands with lime.

Rose's parents suffer financial hardships when their mining venture fails.

Rose supports the family with her sewing and gardening.

In response to her parents' continual insistence on marriage, Rose takes a vow of virginity and joins the third order of St. Dominic.

Making her home in a small hut in the garden, Rose retreats into solitude, wearing a crown of sharp silver thorns on her head to emulate Jesus' crown of thorns.

Rose provides services to her community while suffering greatly with internal anguish.

Rose spends the last three years of her life in the home of Don Gonzolo de Massa and his wife, where Rose endures many painful illnesses.

1617 August 24: Rose dies and is carried to her grave.

1671 Rose is canonized by Pope Clement X as the first saint of the New World.

What will you change in yourself to bring people to Christ?

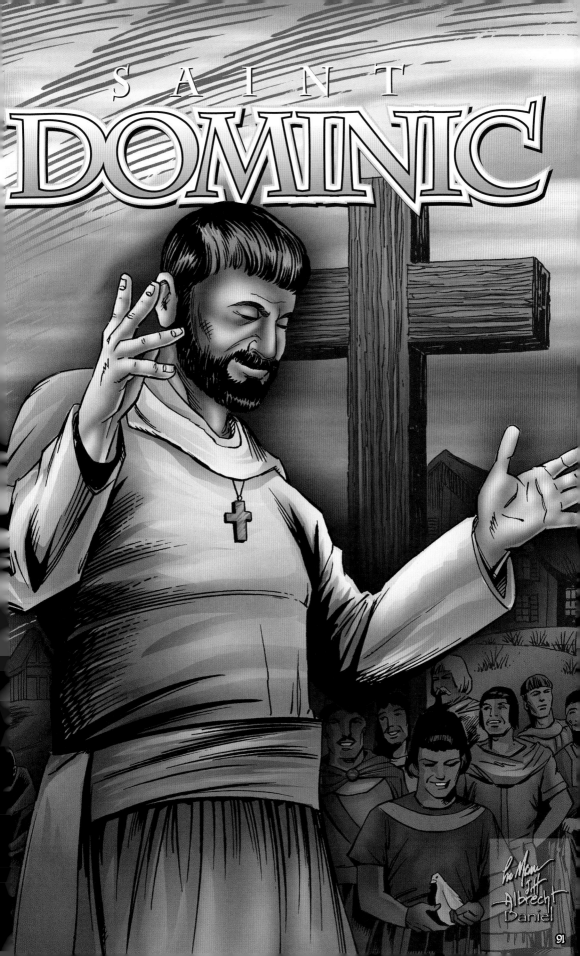

SAINT DOMINIC

"THESE, MY MUCH-LOVED ONES, ARE THE BEQUESTS WHICH I LEAVE YOU AS MY SONS: HAVE CHARITY AMONG YOU; HOLD TO HUMILITY; KEEP WILLING POVERTY."
~ ST. DOMINIC

A PREACHER *UNDETERRED.*

A FOUNDER *UNSHAKEN.*

A FAITH *UNBREAKABLE.*

ST. DOMINIC, *BELOVED PREACHER* AND FOUNDER OF THE *DOMINICAN ORDER,* OTHERWISE KNOWN AS THE ORDER OF PREACHERS, REMAINS A MAN INFLUENTIAL IN ALL CORNERS OF THE EARTH. HIS GREAT LOVE, *UNSTOPPABLE SPIRIT,* AND VISION REALIZED IN HIS OWN TIME HELPED THE CATHOLIC CHURCH TO *OVERCOME* A GREAT THREAT, *RENEWING* THE LIGHT OF TRUTH TO A PEOPLE *LOST IN DARKNESS.*

IN A *WORLD* OF VIOLENCE, HE *PREACHED PEACE.* IN A PLACE OF *SHADOWS,* HE LIT THE LANTERN OF TRUTH. AND IN OUR TIME, HIS *EXAMPLE* CONTINUES TO *SHINE.*

PRODUCER:
DANIEL BURTON

EDITORIAL:
KIMBERLY BLACK

STORY:
JEN MURVIN EDWARDS

PENCILS:
LOU MANNA

INKS:
AL MILGROM

COLORS:
MARK MCNABB

LETTERS & DESIGNS:
KEITH BAHRENBURG

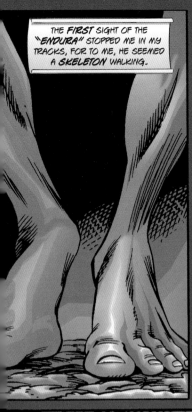

THE *FIRST* SIGHT OF THE "*ENDURA*" STOPPED ME IN MY TRACKS, FOR TO ME, HE SEEMED A *SKELETON* WALKING.

THE *ALBIGENSES* ARE CHRISTIANS WHOSE DOCTRINE HAS *TURNED AWAY* FROM THE *LIGHT OF TRUTH.* BELIEVING THE PHYSICAL WORLD TO BE ONE OF *ULTIMATE CORRUPTNESS* AND EVIL, THEY SEEK TO "*FREE*" THE SOUL FROM ITS MORTAL CAGE -- *THE HUMAN BODY.*

TO ATTAIN THIS *FREEDOM*, THE ALBIGENSES PROMOTE *SUICIDE BY STARVATION*, A PRACTICE KNOWN AS THE "*ENDURA.*"

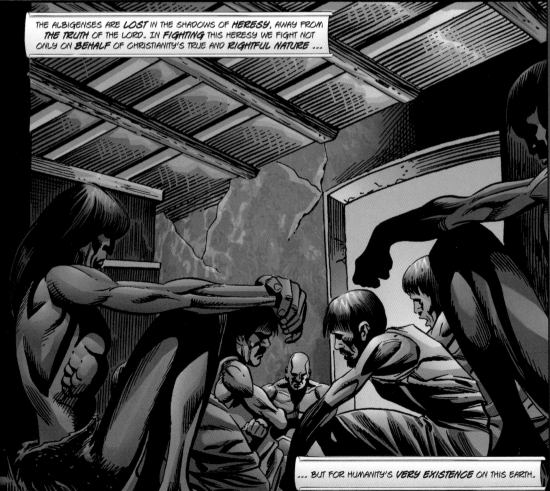

THE ALBIGENSES ARE *LOST* IN THE SHADOWS OF *HERESY*, AWAY FROM *THE TRUTH* OF THE LORD. IN *FIGHTING* THIS HERESY WE FIGHT NOT ONLY ON *BEHALF* OF CHRISTIANITY'S TRUE AND *RIGHTFUL NATURE* ...

... BUT FOR HUMANITY'S *VERY EXISTENCE* ON THIS EARTH.

WE MUST *LEAVE BEHIND* EXCESSIVE PHYSICAL BELONGINGS. WE MUST SEND *OUR HORSES* AND *SERVANTS AWAY*, AS WELL AS ANY SIGN OF *WEALTH*.

WE MUST *CAST OFF* OUR FINERY, WHICH DISTRACTS THE *ALBIGENSES*, AND *REPLACE* IT WITH SIMPLICITY.

THOUGH WE *FEAR* FOR THEIR *SALVATION* AND THEIR LIVES, AND BECOME FRUSTRATED WITH THEIR *MISGUIDED DEEDS*, LET US BE PATIENT.

WE WILL INSTEAD *APPROACH THEM* WITH DISCUSSION AND PERSUASION, *ALWAYS PERSISTENT* ...

ALWAYS PEACEFUL...

1204. PROUILLE. FEAST OF ST. MARY MAGDALEN.

YOU ARE *FLUSHED.* TELL ME, DOMINIO, *WHAT HAS HAPPENED?*

IT BEGAN *LAST NIGHT,* DIEGO, UPON THE FEAST OF *MARY MAGDALEN* ...

I WAS *ASLEEP,* JUST BEFORE DAWN. *SUDDENLY,* I WAS AWAKENED.

IT WAS *A SIGN,* BISHOP -- A SIGN FROM *HEAVEN.*

SO *THIS VISION* YOU HAD LAST NIGHT -- IS *THAT* WHY WE ARE *STANDING HERE,* IN THIS *VACANT FIELD?*

JUST *LOOK BEYOND* THE HORIZON. CAN YOU SEE THEM, *BISHOP DIEGO?*

I CAN *SEE* MY VISION AS IF IT HAS *ALREADY* BECOME REAL -- A VISION OF *HOPE.*

PROUILLE.
1208.

ARE WE ON SCHEDULE?

YES, BROTHER DOMINIC. IN A *MONTH'S TIME* THE CONSTRUCTION OF *THE CONVENT* AND A HOUSE FOR YOUR HELPERS WILL BE COMPLETE. THE *FOUNDING* WILL BE FULFILLED.

THIS *PLACE* WILL SHELTER CONVERTS AND *EDUCATE WOMEN* IN THE TRUE *TEACHINGS OF GOD.*

IT WILL BE A *PERMANENT PLACE* OF PRAYER.

A PLACE TO *TALK TO YOURSELF* AS WELL, I SUPPOSE?

THE *IDLE DAYDREAMS* OF A SIMPLE PREACHER, SISTER.

ALL THIS CONSTRUCTION WOULD *INDICATE* YOU ARE ANYTHING *BUT IDLE,* BROTHER DOMINIC.

COME -- THERE IS *A VISITOR* WHO WISHES TO SEE YOU.

YOU *MUST KNOW* ALREADY WHY I AM HERE, BROTHER. *SURELY* THE NEWS HAS REACHED *EVEN* PROUILLE.

COMMANDER *SIMON*, YOUR PRESENCE *SPEAKS LOUDER* THAN WORDS, BUT NO NEWS HAS REACHED ME WHICH *EXPLAINS* YOUR PRESENCE HERE, IN A *PLACE OF PEACE*.

AN *EVENT* HAS ALTERED OUR *COURSE* -- IT WAS *THE LAST STRAW* FOR THE CATHOLIC CHURCH, AND ROME HAS CALLED *FOR WAR*.

WAR.

IT IS *UNAVOIDABLE* -- WE MARCH UPON THE ENEMY IN JUST UNDER *TWO WEEKS*. THE ALBIGENSES WILL BE *STOPPED* --

BY *FORCE*.

TELL ME, SIMON, WHAT HAS *HAPPENED* TO IGNITE SUCH A *CRUSADE*.

ON A **PEACEFUL** NIGHT, A FIGURE LURKED IN THE **SHADOWS** OF THE DWELLING OF PETER OF **CASTELNAU.**

IT HAS BEEN **CEMENTED** WITH A **DEATH.**

PETER OF CASTELNAU WAS, OF COURSE, THE POPE'S LEGATE AND **A FRIEND.**

POPE INNOCENT III HAD RECENTLY APPEALED TO FRANCE FOR ARMS TO BRING **AGAINST** THE ALBIGENSES; HIS **HOLINESS** WAS PREPARING FOR **ALL SCENARIOS** IN LIGHT OF **THE INFORMATION** HE HAD JUST RECEIVED ...

OVER **1,000** CITIES HAVE BEEN INFILTRATED BY **THE ALBIGENSIAN HERESY.**

PETER OF CASTELNAU HAS BEEN **ASSASSINATED.** POPE INNOCENT III HAS RENEWED HIS APPEAL AND **HIS RESOLVE.**

THE *CRUSADE* HAS BEGUN. THE *ASSASSINATION* HAS BEEN ATTRIBUTED TO ALBIGENSIAN LEADERSHIP. BARONS FROM *NUMEROUS COUNTRIES* HAVE JOINED *OUR CAUSE*.

I WILL LEAD THE *CATHOLIC FORCES* IN THIS WAR. IN THE NAME OF *GOD*, THEY *WILL BE* REDEEMED.

I SEEK *MEN* AND *WOMEN* OF *GOD* WHOSE *LIVES* ARE *DEVOTED* TO THE CONVERSION OF THE *LOST* THROUGH INSTRUCTION AND PATIENCE; THROUGH *TEARS AND PRAYER*.

THOUGH WE *BOTH* WANT THE ALBIGENSIAN *HERESY* DESTROYED, WE DISAGREE ON *HOW* TO GO ABOUT IT. I DO *NOT THINK* VIOLENCE IS THE WAY TO *REDEEM* THESE SOULS, SIMON.

I UNDERSTAND ROME'S *FRUSTRATION*. EVEN *HERE* AT OUR CONVENT WE WAGE WAR FOR *THE SOULS* OF THE ALBIGENSIANS. BUT OUR METHODS ARE *DIFFERENT*, SIMON. HERE WE *SAVE* THESE PEOPLE BY OFFERING THEM *ETERNAL LIFE, NOT DEATH*.

YOUR CONVENT HAS *WEAKENED* THE ENEMY, DOMINIC. PERHAPS MORE THAN *ANY WAR* COULD.

I AM *GLAD* TO HEAR YOU ARE TAKING *STEPS* TO START AN *ORDER*.

AND YET WE *WILL MARCH*. I BEG OF YOU, BROTHER -- *PRAY* FOR US. THOUGH OUR MEANS *DIFFER*, WE *BOTH* SEEK THE *SAME END*. OUR CAUSE IS *ONE*.

I WILL PRAY FOR YOU AND FOR THE *LOST*.

ROME. FOURTH LATERAN COUNCIL.

YOUR HOLINESS, I THANK YOU FOR RECEIVING ME.

DOMINIC, WELCOME. I HAVE HEARD MUCH OF THE SUCCESS OF YOUR CONVENT AT PROUILLE.

I OFFER MY SUPPORT AND ADMIRATION FOR YOUR FORESIGHT IN THIS MATTER.

IT SEEMS THE ALBIGENSIAN WOMEN HAVE BECOME AN INTEGRAL PART OF YOUR CONTINUING MINISTRY AGAINST THIS UGLY HERESY.

MANY THANKS.

I WOULD LIKE YOU TO KNOW THAT I HAVE DRAWN UP A DECREE TO PUT INTO EFFECT THE RESPONSIBILITY OF PREACHING. IT IS UTTERLY ESSENTIAL THAT STRONG MEN, BOTH IN BODY AND FAITH, BE AN EXAMPLE TO ALL WHO HEAR THEM.

YES, I HAVE LONG FELT PASSIONATE ABOUT THE NECESSITY OF PREACHERS IN OUR CAUSE, YOUR HOLINESS.

I KNOW OF YOUR WORK, LAYING A FOUNDATION FOR AN ORDER OF MEN FOR THE PURPOSE OF PREACHING.

I UNDERSTAND YOUR WISH FOR THESE MEN TO CONVERT THOSE ALBIGENSIANS -- AND EVERYONE, FOR THAT MATTER, WHO HAS SURVIVED THE CRUSADE.

THAT IS CORRECT. I SEEK YOUR APPROVAL FOR THE VERY ORDER OF WHICH YOU SPEAK.

THERE ARE DIFFICULTIES -- THIS VERY COUNCIL HAS LEGISLATED AGAINST THE FOUNDING OF NEW RELIGIOUS ORDERS IN THE HOPES OF PROMOTING UNITY.

I DID NOT KNOW THIS, YOUR HOLINESS. I WILL AWAIT YOUR WORD. THE LORD'S WILL BE DONE OVERALL, AND THANK YOU.

I CANNOT GRANT THIS HUMBLE MAN HIS ORDER, BUT LORD, I BESEECH YOU, BLESS HIM IN HIS EFFORTS.

107

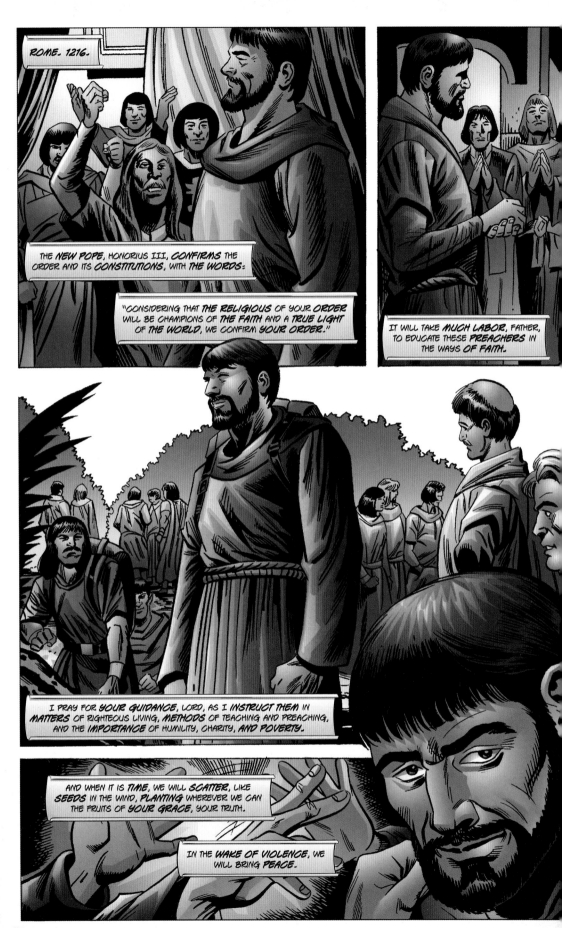

ROME. 1216.

THE *NEW POPE*, HONORIUS III, *CONFIRMS* THE ORDER AND ITS *CONSTITUTIONS*, WITH *THE WORDS:*

"CONSIDERING THAT *THE RELIGIOUS* OF YOUR *ORDER* WILL BE CHAMPIONS OF *THE FAITH* AND A *TRUE LIGHT* OF *THE WORLD*, WE CONFIRM *YOUR ORDER.*"

IT WILL TAKE *MUCH LABOR*, FATHER, TO EDUCATE THESE *PREACHERS* IN THE WAYS OF *FAITH*.

I PRAY FOR *YOUR GUIDANCE*, LORD, AS I *INSTRUCT THEM* IN *MATTERS* OF RIGHTEOUS LIVING, *METHODS* OF TEACHING AND PREACHING, AND THE *IMPORTANCE* OF HUMILITY, CHARITY, *AND POVERTY*.

AND WHEN IT IS *TIME*, WE WILL *SCATTER*, LIKE *SEEDS* IN THE WIND, *PLANTING* WHEREVER WE CAN THE FRUITS OF *YOUR GRACE*, YOUR TRUTH.

IN THE *WAKE OF VIOLENCE*, WE WILL BRING *PEACE*.

PREPARING FOR BATTLE

1170

ST. DOMINIC IS BORN TO *PARENTS* FELIX GUZMAN AND *JOAN OF AZA*, IN *CASTILE*. LITTLE IS KNOWN OF HIS *EARLY CHILDHOOD*.

1184

ST. DOMINIC ENTERS THE *SCHOOL OF PALENCIA* AND IS *LATER* MADE *CANON* OF THE *CATHEDRAL OF OSMA*, WHERE HE RESIDES AFTER HIS ORDINATION. THIS CHAPTER LIVES UNDER *THE RULE* OF ST. AUGUSTINE; *THE VIRTUES* AND CHARACTERISTICS *PROMOTED* IN THIS ENVIRONMENT *INFLUENCE* HIS LIFE GREATLY.

1201

ST. DOMINIC SUCCEEDS BISHOP DIEGO D'AZEVEDO AS *PRIOR* IN OSMA.

1204

ST. DOMINIC ACCOMPANIES *BISHOP DIEGO* ON AN ERRAND TO *NEGOTIATE* A MARRIAGE FOR *ALFONSO IX*, KING OF CASTILE. ON THEIR *JOURNEY*, THE TWO MEN PASS THROUGH LANGUEDOC, A CITY *FILLED* WITH THE HERESY OF *THE ALBIGENSES*. BISHOP DIEGO AND *ST. DOMINIC* RESIDE AT THE HOME OF AN *ALBIGENSIAN BELIEVER*; DURING HIS STAY, ST. DOMINIC *TALKS* WITH THE MAN THROUGHOUT THE NIGHT, *CULMINATING* IN THE MAN'S CONVERSION FROM *THE HERESY*. MANY SAY IT IS AT THIS TIME THAT *ST. DOMINIC* REALIZES GOD'S WILL FOR HIS LIFE: TO *FIGHT* THE *ALBIGENSIAN HERESY*.

1218–1219

ST. DOMINIC *TRAVELS ACROSS SPAIN*, FRANCE, AND *ITALY*, FOUNDING FRIARIES THROUGHOUT THE *COUNTRIES*.

1221

THE SECOND GENERAL CHAPTER OF THE *FRIAR PREACHERS* HAS NOW OVER *SIXTY FRIARIES* IN *EIGHT PROVINCES*. ST. DOMINIC VISITS *VENICE* AND FALLS ILL. KNOWING HE IS IN HIS *FINAL DAYS*, HE SPEAKS TO HIS BROTHERS OF *CHASTITY, CHARITY, HUMILITY, AND POVERTY*.

AUGUST 6, 1221

ST. DOMINIC, NOW TAKEN TO *BOLOGNA* UPON HIS REQUEST, *REPEATS* A PRAYER OF CHASTITY, HUMILITY AND POVERTY, AND *DIES* AT AGE *FIFTY*.

1234

POPE GREGORY IX CANONIZES ST. DOMINIC. IT IS SAID THAT *UPON THIS SIGNING*, POPE GREGORY IX DECLARES THAT HE *"NO MORE DOUBTED THE SANCTITY OF DOMINIC THAN HE DID THAT OF ST. PETER OR ST. PAUL."*

GO!
Make
disciples
of all
nations.

Baptize them in the name of the Father, the Son, and the Holy Spirit.

Teach them to obey everything I have commanded you.

Matthew
28:19-20a

*GO!

Make disciples of all nations.

Baptize them in the name of the Father, the Son, and the Holy Spirit.

Teach them to obey everything I have commanded you.

Matthew 28:19-20a